BUILDING A SUCCESSFUL MARRIAGE:

Effective guide on how to nurture your marriage.

Ellen S. Harris

All rights reserved. No part of this publication may be reproduced, distributed, or transmitted in any form or by any means, including photocopying, recording, or other electronic or mechanical methods, without the prior written permission of the publisher, except in the case of brief quotations embodied in the critical reviews and certain other noncommercial uses permitted by copyright law.

Copyright © Ellen S. Harris, 2022

Table of contents

Chapter 1: HOW TO MAKE YOUR MARRIAGE WORK

Marriage does take work, and like anything different in life, you have to do the work to reap the price. But the work of marriage isn't like drawing the restroom and taking out the trash. What does a successful marriage mean to you? Marriage is a union of two souls, yet the meaning of successful marriage differs from couple to couple. There's no clear description of a successful marriage.

Still, there are some standard delineations of a successful marriage which are :

1. Having a good woman. For some people, a successful marriage means having a good woman. For some, a righteous woman who'll take care of their hubby and

support him at all costs is what makes a marriage successful.

2. Raising a moral family. Some people believe that marriage is the union of two people and the family. They believe as a citizen of society, they need to raise their kiddies innocently and upright. They believe that if they can raise their children right, society will have better people, and for them, it's the description of a successful marriage.

3. One with effective communication. Some people believe that clear communication and fellowship are the keys to a successful marriage. These people are induced that talking to each other without reservation and hiding no secrets makes a marriage successful.

4. Living as musketeers. Still, this might be it, If you're looking for a simple secret to a happy marriage. This is one of the most talked-about delineations of a successful marriage. Some people forcefully believe that participating in life as musketeers is the ultimate key to a successful marriage.

5. Unconditional love and understanding. Another common description of a successful marriage is commitment, responsibility, and immolation. Some people believe that good understanding and unconditional love are the keys to a successful marriage. Accept your mate with excrescences and understand that nothing is perfect.

What are the most important effects of marriage? Still, you must understand the essential effects in marriage that help keep the relationship healthier, If you're looking for the form for a happy marriage.

There are some rudiments of a successful marriage you should consider if you want to fall under happily wedded couples. These are:

1. Respect: There should be collective respect in marriage. Without respect, marriage can be poisonous and stressful. It would help if you excluded anything that can lead your mate to discourteous you and vice versa. Understand your mate's perspective and try to work around that. Having a different opinion but still understanding where your mate is coming from is an excellent way to show your respect towards your mate.

2. Setting Boundaries: Another important key to a successful marriage is setting particular boundaries without vacillation. You should keep an individual life and take out some time for yourself. You may be going on dates for five days a week, but you should also be suitable to meet with your musketeers and family frequently.

3. Trust all successful marriages need collective and unbreakable trust between mates. Although it takes time to make that kind of trust, you have to put in sweat right from the launch.

4. Support: Having a probative mate makes every marriage happy and successful. It's absolutely important to have a mate who believes in you and supports you unconditionally.

21 CRUCIAL SECRETS TO A SUCCESSFUL MARRIAGE

1. Be independent: Independence is highly rated as extremely important in a marriage. To be happy in a relationship, we must be happy first. That is, in fact, the key to a successful relationship. With that in mind, women and misters must continue to take out time for themselves,

enjoy their pursuits, and in general, spend some time piecemeal. Not only does absence make the heart grow fonder, but in the time we spend alone, we get to reunite with our spiritual side, re-establish our sense of tone, and check- in with the progress of our particular preferences, pretensions, and achievements.

On the other hand, being dependent weakens your resoluteness and capability to move forward as a free thinker. When we maintain our independent sense of tone, we will always have a commodity to talk about at the regale table, and we're ever stronger, healthier, and more seductive to our mates.

2. Be a good listener . We need to talk. Most mates dread this judgment but do you know that if you're wondering how to have a successful marriage, also creating a platform for healthy exchanges is the way to go? While all women should work on active listening, we emphasize this as an area of special attention for men. Too frequently, men don't realize that all their mate needs from them is a harkening observance.

This is due to their programming and how they're tutored to relate to others. The flashback shows that harkening and hearing aren't the same effects. Harkening involves our hearts. Open yours, hear what she says, look at her while she speaks, translate indeed, and assure. Harkening is the real key to a happy marriage, for that matter, to every relationship.

3. Agree to differ. Being good together doesn't mean that couples agree on every little thing. Most of the couples we canvassed had varying stations, opinions, and belief systems; and indeed held opposing views on major areas in some cases. All couples should have some position of disagreement. Successful, loving couples admired the

point of view of one another and indeed had a sense of humor over their points of contention. Flashback, respect is one of the major tips for a successful marriage.

4. Communicate. There are several books out there on the Languages of Love. This was developed from the conception in psychology that each existent has its unique way of communicating love. By knowing your mate's preferences and pursuits, conceits can be used to communicate commodities the person understands well. Observe the physical way your mate shows love, and you'll know what makes a successful marriage. This could be washing your auto or picking up the kiddies. It could be keeping the toiletries grazed and ironing his shirts. For others, it's words, letters, and affection. Figure out your mate's love language so you'll always know how to speak to them. Love languages are frequently talked about, but couples don't pay as important attention to this as they should. Understanding a mate's love language is the secret to a happy relationship.

Believe it or not, communication is the key to a happy marriage. Make sure that you always communicate easily about what you want and anticipate. A flashback is that good communication is what makes a marriage successful.

5. Forgive each other. This can be one of the most complex keys to embrace, especially if you generally hold a grudge. This key goes hand- in hand with soliciting together and offering grace. remission is an extension of both of those keys. Take a deep breath and forgive your hubby for not flashing back to stop and snare milk. Forgive your woman for shrinking your shirt. Remission can transfigure your marriage, but it takes time and tolerance with yourself and your mate to look at them and tell them that you forgive them for hurting you in history. But if you can forgive

your mate, you can move forward together without wrathfulness or frustration, and that once pain can begin to heal. Start small if you can and work up to those big situations. Remission is an important tool in marriage and will help you have a more successful marriage this time.

6. Acceptance. A major relationship killer, lack of acceptance, is a particularity more generally attributed to women known for their trouble. Flashback, you married your mate for who he was also and now. Indeed if we wanted to change him now, we can't. The key to a successful marriage lies in realizing this as soon as possible. When prompting or prevailing him, you only concentrate on his sins or problems. Change your perspective incontinently and start fastening on positive traits rather.

7. Take responsibility. It's that easy and one of the secrets of a successful marriage. When you share in a design, take responsibility for your successes and failures. When you and your mate have a disagreement or argument, flashback to take responsibility for your conduct, including anything you did or said, especially if it was hurtful, unthoughtful, or created adversity.

8. Don't take one another for granted. Taking one another for granted may be the most poisonous pathogen of all. Once they're comfortable, it's easy for couples to slip into a perfunctory state – and prospects form. This is only a matter of mortal nature, as we get comfortable with what's familiar, but in marriage, you absolutely should no way come to a place where you take your mate for granted. Pledge to admire your mate indefinitely no matter what. Avoid hypotheticals, and offer to do nice effects for your mate whenever possible.

9. Date night. Among the other tips for a successful marriage, courting is the most ignored and overlooked by couples. It doesn't count what a couple does on their date night. Simply having a night when they spend their time with each other strengthens the bond and maintains it over time. When you have a date night, you should turn your phones off and put them down, so you're free of distractions. Watch a movie at home with popcorn or go hiking or rollerblading together. Change it up frequently and be helpful and cheerful to one another. A romantic and thoughtful date night isn't just one of the ways to a successful marriage. It's important to schedule this yearly, if not daily, to maintain.

10. Go old academy with your love. Romantic acts can be numerous – passing by giving her a flower someday or placing a love note in his briefcase or pack. Surprise him with his favorite mess, or watch the evening together. There's no deficit of marriage tips and ideas, and you'll be amazed at how far a little love goes toward strengthening the relationship.

11. Keeping closeness alive. Coitus is veritably important to a healthy marriage. Coitus should be regular, and therapists suggest doing it indeed when you're not in the mood! We suggest keeping it intriguing by talking about what pleases you and adding any fantasy part- playing, positions, or bedroom props you may want to introduce to keep it instigative. After all, what's a successful marriage if it doesn't let you get what you ask?

12. "A compliment a day keeps the divorce attorney down. " Admitting your mate's positive attributes every day, and paying respects, will go a long way in your connections. Stay positive, and keep track of what your mate does well. When the going gets rough, and his not-so-great attributes

come forward, rather than fastening on the negative, try switching gears, and point out the positive stuff rather.

13. Look for the soft emotion. Behind every " hard " emotion is a soft one; psychologists educate this conception. When we feel wrathfulness, it's generally masking another emotion behind it, similar to sadness, disappointment, or covetousness. We frequently use wrathfulness as a disguise to cover our vulnerabilities. Looking for the " soft " or vulnerable feelings underneath someone's complex display of wrathfulness will help keep you connected as you're better equipped to empathize with that person's genuine emotion. We're frequently searching for marriage tips for a successful relationship. Still, We fail to realize that a simple thing similar to relating the reality of feelings can keep us on the right track.

14. Let go of the fantasy . Unfortunately, we're mingled to believe in fairytale consummations, and we may carry some false perspectives on reality into a majority. We need to fete that, while marriage can be a beautiful thing, it isn't royal, nor will it ever be perfect. Have realistic prospects and don't fall victim to the puck tale – you may find yourself plaintively dissatisfied. This isn't only one of the most important keys to a successful marriage but plays a massive part in your happiness as an individual too.

15. Don't control . Wedded people frequently come to a place where they start to lose themselves, they give in to covetousness or passions of inadequacy, or they forget that they're separate people down from their mates, and they may try to control their mates.

Most of the time, this is done inadvertently, as prospects may grow over time. What makes a marriage successful are communication, independent time, and healthy indulgences that will keep any couple on track. However, get a handle on it or make an appointment for a family counselor, If you smell you're being controlled or are the regulator.

16. Don't use the D- word . Presuming you don't want to get a divorce, don't hang on. Couples using the D- word or talking about separation during fights use this as a control medium. Couples using it threateningly are more likely to see divorce come to consummation.

Making Pitfalls isn't a mature strategy for working on any problem, so don't do it.

17. Supplicate together. This is one of those keys that takes so little time from jam-packed days but gives you space to breathe together.

Before bed, each night or right after you tuck the little bones into bed and say prayers with them, supplicate with your mate.

Take many twinkles to offer thanks and grace to God and each other. These quiet moments when you invite God into your marriage help to strengthen your emotional connection to God and your mate.

18. Offer grace to each other. Still, you're fairly quick to offer grace to the people we work with each day or to our children when they make miscalculations If you're like me.

Too frequently, we hold grievances or harbor wrathfulness with our mates rather than offering them that same grace that flows so fluently in numerous other areas of our lives.

Our mates frequently take the mass of our frustrations and lapses, and we forget that we've to also seek the good in them.

19. Have tolerance for each other. Parenthood books talk about how children frequently bear the worst for their

parents because they're most comfortable and safe at home. The same holds for successful marriages. We frequently show our worst sides to our mates because we're comfortable and safe with them. That can frequently look like frustration and a severe lack of tolerance. We get frustrated when they take ever in the shower or when they aren't home at the exact time they said. Flashback, this is the person you love most in the world. Grant them the same tolerance you grant to your toddler at the veritably least.

20. Admire each other(in private and in public)

One of the loftiest respects you can give to another person is to have them hear that you have been singing their praises to others when they aren't indeed there. When you're out and about professionally or socially, admire your mate by singing their praises in exchanges. Also, admire your mate through your conduct, both in public and private. Still, be home by 5(as frequently as you can), If you said you would be home by 5. Still, admire your mate enough to call, If you're running late. In private, admire your mate by speaking to them as if they count on you. Sing their praises in front of your children. Hear them when they tell you about their day. It's such a simple gesture, and it matters.

21. Encourage each other. It's important to know your mate's priorities and dreams. This new time is a great time to talk about your pretensions. When your mate shares their pretensions and judgments with you, please encourage them to negotiate them. Make their pretensions as necessary as your own. Be their biggest cheerleader, and do your stylist to help them and give them the space they need to meet their pretensions for the time. This also works for the pretensions you set together. How can you

push and support each other to be the stylish interpretation of yourselves that you can be? Make your existent and couple pretensions precede and celebrate your progress throughout the time.

More Tips For A Successful And Healthy Marriage

" Success in marriage doesn't come simply through changing the right mate, but through being the right mate. " – Barnett. Brickner

At first, when we've nothing but each other, we concentrate hard on the important structure blocks of a healthy and successful marriage. But as our relationship continues forward, " stuff " begins to accumulate and begins to distract us from the veritable rudiments of what makes a good marriage.

Suddenly, we worry more about the appraisal value of our home than the value of our relationship. We check the health of our withdrawal account far more frequently than the health of our marriage. Or we spend further time taking care of the auto in the garage than the other person in our bed. Effects begin to accumulate in our homes and lives and soon demand our plutocrats, energy, and precious time. As a result, we've little left over for minding the very rudiments of a happy marriage.

Wise couples realize that a nice home, auto, or withdrawal account may appear nice to have, but they don't make a successful marriage. They understand that there are far more important principles at play. They've learned to invest their plutocrat, energy, and time into the rudiments of a healthy marriage.

- Love/ Commitment.

At its core, love is a decision to be committed to another person. It's far further than a transitory emotion as portrayed on TV, the big screen, and in love novels. passions come and go, but a true decision to be committed lasts ever — and that's what defines healthy marriages.

Marriage is a decision to be committed through the ups and the campo, the good and the bad. When the effects are going well, commitment is easy. But true love is displayed by remaining committed indeed through the trials of life.

- Sexual fantasies.

Sexual fastness in marriage includes further than just our bodies. It also includes our eyes, mind, heart, and soul. When we devote our minds to sexual fantasies about another person, we immolate sexual fastness to our partner. When we offer moments of emotional familiarity to another, we immolate sexual fastness to our partner. Guard your fornication daily and devote it entirely to your partner. Sexual fastness requires tone- discipline and mindfulness of the consequences. Refuse to put anything in front of your eyes, body, or heart that would compromise your fastness.

- Humility.

We all have sins and connections always reveal these faults more hastily than anything differently on earth. An essential structural block of a healthy marriage is the capability to admit that you aren't perfect, that you'll make miscalculations, and that you'll need remission. Holding a station of superiority over your mate will bring about resentment and will help your relationship from moving forward. Still, snare a pencil and snappily write down three effects that your mate does better than you — that simple exercise should help you stay humble If you struggle in this area.

- Tolerance/ remission.

Because no one is perfect, tolerance and remission will always be needed in a marriage relationship. Successful marriage mates learn to show everlasting tolerance and remission to their mate. They submissively admit their faults and don't anticipate perfection from their mate. They don't bring up crimes in trouble to hold their mate hostage. And they don't seek to make amends or get vengeance when miscalculations occur. However, forgive him or her, If you're holding onto a once hurt from your mate. It'll set your heart and relationship free.

- Time.

Connections don't work without the time investment. No way have, no way will. Any successful relationship requires purposeful, quality time together. And quality time infrequently happens when volume time is absent. The relationship with your partner should be the most intimate and deep relationship you have. Thus, it's going to bear further time than any other relationship. However, set away time each day for your partner, If possible. And a date night formerly in a while wouldn't hurt moreover.

- Honesty and Trust.

Honesty and trust come as the foundation for everything in a successful marriage. But unlike most of the other rudiments on this list, trust takes time. You can come selfless, married, or case in a moment, but trust always takes time. Trust is only erected after weeks, months, and times of being who you say you're and doing what you say you'll do. It takes time, so start now and if you need to rebuild trust in your relationship, you'll need to work indeed harder.

- Selflessness.

Although it'll no way show up on any check, further marriages are broken up by egoism than any other reason. checks condemn it on finances, lack of commitment, infidelity, or incompatibility, but the root cause for the utmost of these reasons is egoism. A selfish person is committed only to himself or herself, shows little tolerance, and no way learns how to be a successful partner. Give your expedients, dreams, and life to your mate. And begin to live life together. This is a simple call to value our marriages, treat them with great care, and invest in them daily.

Numerous couples could avoid divorce if they got some good advice(and flashed back it) when their marriage started having serious trouble. Then there are some tips that should benefit the utmost couples. Suppose before you speak. Couples tend to develop hot button issues that beget frequent arguments. You can reduce bickering by staying before responding to a commodity that has made you angry. Count to ten. It may be better to bandy delicate issues formerly feelings aren't so high.

Do not give up. Any wedded person will tell you that marriages wax and wane. There are good times, bad times, and so-so times. A marriage is feasible if the good outweighs the bad, indeed by a little bit. The more you appreciate the good and try to let the bad roll off, the easier it'll get, and the more fondness and connection you'll feel towards your partner.

Give your marriage at least as important attention as you give your pursuits. People spend huge quantities of time, plutocrats, and trouble on their off-work interests. But when a marriage is making them feel bad, some throw up their hands and decide that it's useless to try presently.

Reading books on marriage, conflict resolution, and communication ways will help your marriage. Getting your partner to read them is indeed better.

Treat your partner better than you treat anyone differently. Have you heard the expression" familiarity types disdain?" The unfortunate variety is that people tend to treat their consorts worse than they treat nonnatives. Retrain yourself to give your partner the utmost respect.

Have separate interests.

Make sure you have some private space, and give your partner some, too. Marriage entails a lot of togetherness, but you do not need to be joined at the hipsterism.

Encourage your partner's dreams and pretensions. In a successful marriage, one partner is happy about the other's successes. Good consorts foster the other in achieving pretensions. occasionally pretensions, similar to a career change, are scary and need to be precisely estimated. Do the work together.

Find effects you enjoy doing together. A marriage is a partnership. However, you'll ultimately grow piecemeal, If you both have completely separate interests. Find participating interests, hobbies, and enjoyment, feeling that this conditioning will presumably change over time.

Do not suppose the lawn is always greener on the other side. Most people who leave their marriages for someone differently find the same problems in the new relationship, and numerous remorse for not having worked effects out in their first marriage.

Do not sweat the little effects. As in the world of work, it's important to have precedents. Precisely pick your battles, and let the other stuff slide. Congratulate your partner at least formally every day. This leads to a healthy relationship, and it's the right thing to do because your partner is presumably doing numerous good effects every day.

Work hard with your partner to produce fiscal security. One of the benefits of marriage is the creation of a strong profitable common adventure. As your fiscal security builds up, it'll be one of the effects that let you feel good about each other and the world. It'll also be a measure of the good work you've both done during your marriage.

Be your partner's mate. Keep each other informed about the conditioning you're engaged in, including your work days and what you do at home. The time you spend independently outdoors in the world every day is veritably significant. Always talk to each other at the end of the day about how your day went.

Always assume the stylist of your partner. Everyone has misconstructions and miscommunications. However, stay a bit and, also, If your partner's conduct affects you. You might well find that your partner meant to be formative and not negative and that you made the wrong interpretation or supposition.

Give your partner a treat occasionally.However, offer it without being asked occasionally, indeed if you do not watch for it If there is a commodity your partner likes. It can be a small thing a date to the pictures, a lift to a place your partner likes to go, or perhaps a favorite food from the grocery store

Do not fight with your partner about the kiddies. dissensions about children can be veritably sharp in a marriage. Have your conversations offline so that your children don't know you differ. Get professional advice, if demanded, to help you coordinate and admire your different views.

Do not complain about your partner to your musketeers and family. One complaint at a low time in your marriage will reverberate with the listener long after the problem or wrangle was resolved. However, find an independent professional, If you need to talk with someone about your marriage.

Be faithful. Affairs destroy numerous marriages. However, be honest with everyone and end the marriage first, If you can not repel someone outside of your marriage.

Spend time with collective musketeers. Pursuing outside gemütlichkeit together, with single people or other couples, is frequently veritably good for a marriage.

Forgive each other. Marriage is veritably long, and bad effects are bound to be. Every partner(indeed you!) makes miscalculations and treats the other inadequately at times. You must be suitable to forgive your partner for the wrongs done to you and move on. Flashback that the coming time it may be you who needs to be forgiven.

Appreciate each other's benefactions to the connubial adventure. Marriages frequently fail because of perceived differences in the position of donation of each party. Try to appreciate the other person's benefactions, whether they're fiscal or emotional. Marriage is not easy. Erecting a strong marriage takes time, trouble, and maturity. But it's worth it. Here are also some principles for a successful marriage.

1. ACCEPT THE NOTION THAT THERE WILL BE STORMS.

All marriages have difficulties. Honeymoons end and the cute stuff starts to look(and sound) disgusting. Accepting the idea that marriage isn't a disney happily-ever-later movie, will help open the door to a life that can be plushly satisfying. Real life, after all, can't contend with the Disney true-love, soul-mate fantasy. And to the degree that's the anticipation and the measure, we simply won't end up looking veritably good.

2. WEATHER THE STORMS, ENDURE THE PROBLEMS

You have to be devoted to marriage itself, as an institution, maybe as important as to the person you're wedded to. That way, in those trying times, there will be some holding power. A storm is not a failure. It's just a storm. occasionally all you need to do is let it pass.

3. CARE

The stylish drug is an ounce of forestallment. So the stylish way to keep the honey of love from dying is to keep it alive. Don't let effects poach on low for too long. Don't get lazy and start throwing your undergarments in the corner of the room or leave your hair in the Gomorrah. Don't let yourself take each other for granted.

4. KEEP THE LOVE ALIVE

Date night. Just do it. We've had times when date nights were regular and we've had ages when date nights kept getting shoved off to the eternal " coming time. " The difference has been stark. Clinch and hold hands, open doors, leave notes for each other and give back aggravations and shoulder massages. Treat each other as though you were deeply in love, and you'll likely remain deeply in love.

5. MARRIAGE IS NO BIG DEAL; IT 'S A BUNCH OF LITTLE BONES

Have you allowed " please " and " thank you " to drop from your exchanges with each other? Have you stopped holding the door for her? Have you stopped running to give him a clinch when he comes home? When was the last time you told your partner you loved and appreciated him or her? When was the last time you played a board game or had a pierce fight or took a walk around the block hand in hand? Don't let the little effects slide or you'll probably have a bigger mess to clean up later.

6. PASSION COUNTS

Hear her passions. They won't make sense to you. Hear anyway. They will feel illogical and maddening. Hear anyway. passions make sense to the person feeling them(generally). Validating those passions is a sign of respect. And respect is a necessary element of sustained love.

7. SERVICE

Clean up the house, make breakfast in bed, wash the others ' auto, and bring home his/ her favorite CD or book. By serving with a willing heart, out of a desire to do a commodity kind for the other, you develop lesser love and compassion for that person. And you inspire in that person an appreciation for your service, the sense that they are loved.

8.PRIORITIZE YOUR PARTNER Still, your marriage will be at the end of the list too, If you put your partner at the end of every list. You can't see your partner as an extension of yourself. You're different people with different requirements and personalities. Treat each other as similar.

9. WORK ON YOUR LOVE

Character matters. So work on your tolerance, compassion, remission, selflessness, modesty, and love. The further similar traits that you have, the lesser your capacity to love. egoism and pride are the binary destroyers of love. Work daily at prostrating these venoms.

10. LEARN YOUR PARTNER 'S LANGUAGE

According to Dr. Craig Giorgiana, we all have one of three primary love languages.

Some are acquainted. They express their love by doing effects for others. That's how they admit it as well. Others are verbal. Telling them how important you love them is crucial. They need to hear it. Those who are touch acquainted express and " hear " love through touch, in the form of a clinch, holding hands, a touch.

Forcing others into your particular favored mode of communication is a losing proposition. But learning their language will prepare you to be suitable to shoot dispatches of love loud and clear.

Still, you'll deliver the communication you meant to deliver, no matter how sincere the delivery. If you keep speaking Swahili to your partner who only speaks Cantonese.

11. DON'T SINK THE BOAT

Certain deal-combers can incontinently end a relationship. Avoid them like a pest. Stay down from indeed the appearance of these deal-breakers. However, run! Fast! The destruction isn't worth the emotional release at the moment If the temptation arises.

Infidelity, any form of abuse of anyone in the family, crime, and medicine, are all similar acts of misprision, disdain, and casualness for the others in the family that warrant a dissolution and indeed legal remedies. The person engaged in any of this conditioning clearly needs help. But immolating yourself or your children in the process of " being there " is an inferior way to deliver that help.

Chapter 2: NURTURING YOUR MARRIAGE

Currently, a lot of couples are hysterical about tying the knot because divorce has come so normal in ultramodern society. Everyone expects all connections are fated to end one day, so why go through the hassle of legalizing effects?

Still, there are some ways to nurture your marriage and make it stronger, If you're among the stalwart couples who have taken the threat of bringing their relationship to the coming position. Here are some ways:

1. Set a regular date.

Indeed if you're past the courting stage, it's still important that you have your regular " babe time ". Just like how important quality time was when you were only starting together, it is still important now to stay together. Make it a point to go out on a date at least once a week.

2. Do your pursuits together.

To nurture your marriage, find a common pastime that you can do with each other, like hiking, playing a sport, gardening, or oil. Having the same interests will give you a commodity pleasurable to talk about and look forward to together, which is necessary to ameliorate your bond.

3. Take time to talk about your day.

No matter how busy your diurnal routines are, see to it that you can still have time to sit down together and get updates about each other's day. It can be the coffee time in the morning or a not-so-late night talk in bed before closing your eyes.

4. Produce your marriage core values.

Consorts may have different principles and societies, but by setting core values for marriage and family, these differences can be confirmed. The hubby and woman need to sit down together to establish norms for the family. In any case, you can agree on recognizing each other in front of the kiddies, so they mustn't see you arguing.

5. Set marriage pretensions together.

Marriage isn't the final destination. Indeed as a wedded couple, your relationship has still a lot to grow. To nurture your marriage, set pretensions for your marriage to be productive. For illustration, you can aim for a healthy life, so you'll make it a habit to drill together. You may also target a specific quantum for savings.

6. Don't leave celebrating special occasions.

Don't forget about special dates, similar to your marriage anniversary or each other's birthday. Indeed a simple festivity would mean a lot as long as you commemorate the significance of the occasion together, or with the rest of the family.

7. Go on a monthly vacation trip.

Have commodity instigatives to look forward to in your marriage. Make it a thing to travel together at least formerly a time. The cling and recollections you'll produce would surely keep your relationship as hubby and woman solid. This is also a time for both of you to decompress and estimate your marriage and life together.

8. Don't suggest separation as a result of any problem.

It's normal for conflicts to arise in marriage. Still, if you don't want to add to the marriage mortality rate, don't suggest separation or divorce. Staying in a decision, so as long as you both are willing to make it work, no way to give up on each other no matter how rough it gets.

9. Always make trouble to keep the passion burning.

Love and closeness are the spices that keep a marriage instigative. Thus, indeed if your marriage is past the magnet stage, both of you should make trouble to keep the passion between you alive. Always do commodities to keep your mate attracted to you and agitated to be with you.

10. Let your appreciation be known to each other.

Feeling ungrateful is one of the reasons that can alienate a relationship. Indeed in small effects, make it a habit to appreciate and express gratefulness to each other. Away from " I love you ", " thank you " should be the words that must be present in your exchanges daily. Always remind your mate how thankful you're that he is your partner.

11. Be generous with leverages and kisses.

Physical contact is necessary for showing affection.Don't get tired of kissing and embracing your mate. Also, leverages are known to help people be relieved from stress, so giving your partner super leverages would do him or her a lot of virtuousness.

12. Help each other be physically seductive.

Let us face it, falling out of love is occasionally caused by being attracted to someone new — someone youngish, fresher, and more seductive. As you grow older together, it isn't surprising if the time would come that you would not find each other beautiful and handsome presently. To avoid this from passing, encourage each other to take care of yourselves. This would also keep you from being insecure because of the changes brought by age to your constitution.

13. Be the number one supporter of each other.

One of the ways to keep your marriage stronger is by having each other's reverse. further than anyone else, your partner should be your stylish friend, number one addict, and encourager. Be probative of each other's dreams, no matter how high they feel.

14. Choose to talk about problems position-headedly.

Whenever there are problems or conflicts, avoid talking when one or both of you're still at the peak of your emotion, like wrathfulness. Let the situation cool down first to avoid yelling at each other, blurting out hurtful words, making abrupt opinions, and indeed hurting each other physically. Decide to talk when both of you're ready to come up with practical and right results.

15. Make God the center of your marriage.

Faith in God is one of the strongest foundations of marriage . However, also inviting Him to your home should be your first step, If you believe that He's the author and protection of marriage. Make it a habit to supplicate regularly as hubby and woman, read and partake in God's word with each other, and serve Him together. This is a good culture that should include the rest of your family too.

16. Be purposeful

Still, you need to be purposeful with your time and your conduct, If you want to foster growth in your relationship. Sculpt out time to spend with your partner and make sure you're using the time wisely. Indeed if you can only manage a quick twenty or thirty twinkles each day, you need to devote time to your mate.

There are many ways you can be purposeful with your time:

Start a daily date night

Go on a brief walk together after work

Cook breakfast together in the morning

Find a television show you both enjoy and watch it together
Meet for lunch once a week
Find conditioning that you enjoy together

Still you choose to spend time together, make sure that you concentrate on your mate. Make sure to silence your phone, get relieved of any interruptions, and hire a sitter if necessary.
Show your mate that you prioritize your relationship by earmarking time to erect your connection.
17. Show Appreciation
Still, it can be easy to take your mate for granted, If you aren't careful. One of the easiest ways to avoid this is by showing appreciation every single day. suppose of everything, big and small, that your mate does for you each day. Write these conduct down and make sure you don't neglect to thank your mate for doing them.
These are some ideas to get you started :
Write a sincere letter expressing how your partner's selflessness makes you feel
Buy them chocolates, flowers, or some other commemorative appreciation
Say " thank you! "
Take on one of the jobs or chores they generally do for a day
Prepare a romantic regale
Tell other people in your life how important you appreciate your mate
When your mate feels appreciated, it'll nurture your relationship. Nothing kills a relationship briskly than having one person feel like they aren't appreciated or valued. Make it a habit to show appreciation every day.

18. Acts Of Service

Giving is one of the most important acts you can do in a relationship. Take time to complete acts of service for your partner. Does he detest taking the trash out or washing the dishes? Does this chore for him from time to time? Does she put the kiddies to bed every night or always cook regale? Take over this responsibility so that she can have a break. These little acts of service can make a big difference in a relationship.

Laboriously look for areas in which you can help your partner. However, take it to an auto marshland, If you notice your partner's auto is dirty. However, wake up beforehand and prepare a nice breakfast, If you know your significant other has an important meeting. Acts of service are a great way to show your mate you watch about your relationship.

19. Take Responsibility

When you and your mate have a problem or an argument, make sure you take responsibility for your part of the situation. Avoid playing the blame game or making defenses. hear what your significant other has to say without being protective. Also, apologize if applicable and take responsibility for your conduct. Still, make sure you're willing to admit to and enjoy your miscalculations If you want your relationship to flourish.

20. Give Emotional Support

Demonstrate to your mate that you care by showing emotional support. When your mate knows that you have his or her reverse, it'll increase the trust, connection, and love in your relationship.

Hear, give respect and appreciate

There are some easy ways you can make showing emotional support a habit

Offer your loved one respect and confirmation

Hear when they've got a struggle they're facing at work

Ask them how they're doing

Make sure your mate knows they aren't alone in this relationship.

21. Forgive

Holding grievances can be mischievous in any relationship. Get in the habit of forgiving your mate when you have talked through a problem where they were at fault.

Occasionally couples will bring up resolved issues and once miscalculations when they've got an argument. This chips down at the trust in a relationship and prevents you from ever truly working problems. Exercise remission and let go of resolved conflicts.

22. Share

When you partake in your pretensions, dreams, ups, and campo with your mate, you'll come closer. participating is a form of closeness that comes with numerous benefits. You need to be vulnerable and talk about effects that might make you uncomfortable.

Not only does this help your mate know what's going on in your head, but it also allows you to have important discussions. However, you must communicate that with your mate, If your dream is to bear moving across the country or investing time or plutocrat.

23. Perseverance

Like anything worth having, connections bear hard work to maintain. It doesn't count how close you're with your mate; you're going to need to work on your relationship to maintain its integrity. One way you can nurture your relationship is to laboriously work toward perfecting your relationship.

Always be willing to ameliorate, both for your own sake and your mate's. also put in the hard work toward fixing these problem areas. When effects get tough in your relationship, resolve not to give up right down or avoid having hard exchanges. Work on your cooperation in good times and in bad times.

24. Attend Marriage Conferences

Still, consider a couples remedy, If you want to make sure your relationship is as healthy as possible. Couples' remedies can help you work out issues, develop positive habits, and learn to communicate. Try to attend marriage conferences regularly, indeed when you feel like your relationship is solid. Marriage remedies can equip you with the tools and strategies you need to have a successful relationship.

Chapter 3: CAUSES OF MARITAL CONFLICTS

Have you ever asked yourself, "Why is marriage so hard?" If yes, then you should know that it is common marital problems such as these that make marriage tough. All marriages are impacted by problems. Connubial problems beget couples to seek a divorce on a diurnal basis. Whether or not a marriage survives when a problem hits depends on the problem and how a couple decides to deal with that problem. Couples who are suitable to work together in resolving conflict are more likely to be suitable to save their marriage. Couples who warrant the proper conflict resolution chops may find themselves in divorce court for problems that could have fluently been answered.

Consider how you're presently dealing with these issues, and how you could deal more with these issues for the sake of your marriage.Now that you know the most common marital problems, it is important to identify the causes of such problems as well.

The common causes of marital problems include –

1. Miscommunication

One of the most common causes of marital problems includes lack of communication or miscommunication. If you are unclear about your feelings, boundaries, and expectations in your marriage, you are likely to encounter marital problems.

2. Unrealistic expectations

Not having clear expectations about the marriage, the partnership, or how things work between the two of you can also lead to marital troubles.

3. Lack of privacy

If you and your partner go out of the relationship and discuss every aspect of it with parents, children, friends, or even siblings, it could cause marital problems. Your relationship does not have to be a secret, but some matters should be private between just the two of you.

4. Arguments

If you and your spouse only argue and never discuss the problems you are experiencing, it could become a huge cause of marital discord.

5. Dishonesty

If you and your partner are not honest about your feelings, if you lie or hide things from each other, it could cause marriage problems.

6. Plutocrat problems.

Most couples argue over bills, debt, spending, and other fiscal issues. How you decide to deal with plutocratic problems in your marriage will determine whether those problems have a negative or positive effect on your marriage. Still, Jane and Dick are going to face having to resolve the problem of Jane's precious taste and Dick's low income. If Jane loves Gucci shoes and Dick has a blue collar job. I wouldn't put plutocrat on Dick winning that argument and further than likely, Jane has poor conflict resolving chops. I am sure that Jane will be dissatisfied when she finds out that alimony is hard to get these days and indeed if she did, it wouldn't cover the cost of a new brace of Gucci sandals.

7. Children.

Discipline, diet, and other parenthood issues can be sources of disagreement between couples. A child is the number one stressor in a marriage and can accentuate differences in beliefs on issues like how to punish, who's responsible for utmost of the child care or what educational options to choose. And, there's the matter of lost sleep, who has to change dirty diapers, run after them when they start walking and the extravagant cost of daycare. It's easy to see who children can put a strain on indeed the stylish marriage.

8. Coitus.

Frequence, volume, quality, and infidelity are all common sources of stress and discord in a marriage. Withholding coitus to discipline a partner, breaks the connubial bond. Cheating on a partner destroys trust. Coitus can be a HUGE issue when it comes to undoing the promises you took. Coitus is awful until it is not presently!

9. Time piecemeal.

Time piecemeal and a lack of quality time together causes couples to come out of sync with each other. Having participated interests and conditioning you share on a regular basis helps couples stay connected. Military couples fall victim to this problem in their marriages. Enduring long deployments and constant temporary assignments down from home couples have to have a special bond for a marriage to last.

10. Household liabilities.
Numerous couples argue over the indifferent distribution of ménage work, and how to do it. Rather of sitting down and dividing ménage chores fairly they quibble over who did or did n't do what. Do not quibble or divide up chores, you are grown-ups, if you see a commodity that needs to be done, do it. Or, decide together to resolve ménage chores grounded on those you each enjoy or can tolerate the stylish.

11. Musketeers.
Not all musketeers are helpful to connections, some of them are poisonous. Be sure you know the difference between a friend who'll enhance your relationship and one who'll break it down.

12. Prickly habits.
Numerous people are married to someone who has one or further habits they find undesirable. My partner got angry with me. I ask him formerly why and told him there had to be effects I did that bothered him. He responded by telling me he " loved everything about me. " This was shortly before he decided he no longer loved me! So, don't be hysterical to point out habits that irritate you, just be sure you do it in anon-defensive way.

13. Family.

In- laws, siblings, children and step- children can all produce stress within a marriage. When managing negative issues because of family, step gently. Our partner should come first but there are times you have to be willing to take a backseat and suck your lingo.

14. Prospects.

We all go into marriage with certain prospects. Most of the time, marriage is the contrary of what we anticipated. We glamorize marriage and come disillusioned once those romantic prospects aren't met. Unmet prospects are a major source of conflict in marriages.

15. Personality conflicts.

Is your personality ruining your marriage? There are personality traits that can doom a marriage to failure. Are you a conflict avoider? Do you like to " one- up" your partner? Do you bend over backward to please your partner, neglecting your requirements in the process? If you answered yes to any of these, you need to work on changing these negative personality traits.

Chapter 4:HOW TO PREDICT DIVORCE

Divorce rates in the United States have caused concern since the'80s, despite eventually being on the decline. The puzzlingly high chance of marriages that end in divorce, still, has pushed experts to study the causes of this miracle.

There are lots of actions that can predict a divorce from the most egregious bones , like a cheating hubby who can not keep his pants on, to the most confusing bones, like having a son.

Yes, this is one of the strongest predictors of divorce, according to the rearmost studies.

0 seconds of 1 nanosecond, 19 seconde volume 90

We frequently hear that half of all couples divorce, but the real figures aren't that grim.

In reality, one-third of the wedded couples get a divorce and a precious agreement, which can be avoided, if you work on avoiding the reasons for divorce.

1. Carrying on virtual connections

Numerous believe that online courting does not count as an affair, as long as there are no physical meetings. The grim reality is that a cyber-relationship leads to divorce, as the emotional impact of such a relationship is identical to that of physical infidelity.

2. Spending too much on the marriage

Plutocracy is surely one of the major causes of fights and divorce in couples, so is it any wonder why spending too much on marriage puts a strain on the new relationship?

3. Where you live

A study conducted by professor Jennifer Glass, from the University of Texas, set up that divorces are more frequent in the red countries. Unexpectedly, this means divorces are more frequent in further religious areas(suppose Arkansas) than in further liberal bones (suppose New York or New Jersey).

4. Your education position

While one might suppose that a couple without pupil debt is likely to be happier, there are still problems that accompany not pursuing advanced education. Couples with high academic education are more likely to get a divorce, compared to their council-educated peers. The sense behind this is that council education comes with better plutocrat operation chops and advanced paid jobs, which reduce the quantum of fights over plutocrats in the relationship.

5. A long commute

A study set up that divorce rates were advanced among couples who had long commutes. Spending further than 45 twinkles on the way home from work seems to add a lot of stress to a relationship.

6. Having a son

This is presumably the strangest cause of a divorce, but once you understand the sense behind it, it makes sense. According to a study, couples who had boys were less likely to disjoin, compared to couples who had daughters. This is because the mama wants to set a good example for her son, which motivates her to disjoin when the relationship turns sour.

7. Too important social media

When the mates use social media too much, there's an advanced chance they will wind up decoupling. The reason is simple relish prints of a partner, opening on an old crush's profile, or flirting online all tend to destabilize a relationship. Some attorneys claim Facebook alone constitutes a great deal of the divorces they see.

8. Not unyoking the housework unevenly

This bone is a classic for prognosticating divorce. However, with all the laundry and cuisine, you are going to get sick of it one day, If your mate is staying with you to do all the cleaning.

Depending on where you live, you might want to talk about participating in ménage duties with your mate, so you do not end up begrudging them before ultimately calling it quits.

9. The bridegroom had pre-wedding jitters.

If the unbornMrs. has cold bases, the couple's threat of divorce more than doubles, according to a study published in the Journal of Family Psychology. The good news? A bachelor with" I do" doubts has nearly no impact on the future of the marriage.

10. The couple got wedded youthful — or after age 32.

Sure, conventional wisdom holds that getting wedded too beforehand is not the stylish bet for a lasting union." I frequently see couples in their 40s in comfort who got married too youthful and did not have experience with other mates or want different effects now," says Rachel Sussman, a certified psychotherapist and relationship expert." Because there is a veritably good chance that in 10 or 15 times, you are going to be a veritably different person — and
you should be."

But a new study says that after age 32, a couple's threat of divorce increases by 5 each time they stay to wed. Sussman attributes this to settled independence and a need for space.

11. A family has two daughters.

Surely, it ups your chances to 43. And indeed just having one son makes you 5 more likely to resolve, according to Columbia University economist Kristin Mammen. Parents with two sons, in discrepancy, face a nearly 37% threat." We suppose it happens because fathers get further invested in a family life when they've boys," Stephanie Coontz, author of Marriage, a History, and director of the exploration for the Council on Contemporary Families, told The Daily Beast.

12. Divorce runs in the family, so to speak.

Still, you are at least 40% more likely to do the same, If your parents disassociated. But if they got married, you have a stunning 91 liability of getting disassociated.

13. A grueling child challenges a marriage.

Parents who deal with a child's ADHD opinion are nearly 23 more likely to disjoin before the child turns 8.

14. Debt.

Plutocrat straits are an egregious connubial stressor. Not only do numerous divorce threat factors relate to poverty, but connubial happiness dramatically decreases as couples do not pay off their debts or take on new bones . And when one person is the big fritterer, according to one study, divorce can be 45% more likely. (Only adulterous affairs and substance abuse were stronger predictors!)

" There can be a problem when one mate works at a workshop or just has a significantly bigger payment, and the other spends an extravagant amount on a plutocrat. Fighting over the Amex bill every month is just a dumb fight to have. They have got to be on the same runner, and I suppose setting a budget is crucial," explains Sussman.

15. The bachelor lowered in his nonage shots.

In two separate studies, psychologists estimated peoples' nonage and yearbook prints and also estimated their current connubial health. Their findings? People who glare in prints are five times more likely to disjoin than people who smile. (Yes, this one especially, well, far- brought.)

16. One mate smokes but the other doesn't.

When only one person in a relationship smokes, they are 75 to 91 more likely to resolve than smokers who are married to another smoker. Why?" Different values and cultures can be problematic," says Sussman.

17. The family's first child was born less than 8 months after the marriage.

So, a shotgun form is intimately not a stylish way to start your union. But did you know it makes you 24 more likely to call it quits?

18. The couple shacked up before marriage.

Sure, cohabitation has been credited for dwindling the number of divorces overall. (One proposition is that because couples who might otherwise disjoin test the waters and sizzle beforehand, the couples who do marry are more married.). But it's still not inescapably helpful once you do wed. Multiple studies say living together-nuptials gives couples about a 12% higher probability that their marriage will fail.

19. One mate is a nanny.

Yes, certain occupations have advanced divorce rates, and not just the police and military labor force. hop and choreographers have a 43 divorce rate, according to a 2009 study in the Journal of Police and Criminal Psychology. Bartenders resolve from a partner 38 of the time, while nursing, psychiatric, and home health helpers face a nearly 29 divorce rate.

20. You live in Nevada. Or Maine.

While important has been made of" red countries" vs." blue countries" and connubial trends, it's not so simple. Some countries have youngish periods of marriage, lower inflows, and other demographic factors that contribute to the divorce threat. But Nevada residents can presumably just thank Las Vegas for their 14.6 rate of separated people. Maine is alternate with14.2; Oklahoma trails at

13.5. New York, in discrepancy, may only have8.8 separated residers, but it also has one of the smallest numbers of wedded residers. To explain, some experimenters say that you are more likely to get disassociated in utmost" red countries" but only because you are also more likely to get wedded there.

.

21. The woman makes further plutocrats than the hubby. Marriages, where consorts earn roughly the same quantum, are more prone to divorce than those where the woman earns less, according to a Swiss study ofU.S. couples. And if the woman makes 60 or further of the family income, the threat of divorce is double that of couples where she does not work at all.

22. Or she's aged than him.

Unfortunately, women who are one to three times older than their sisters are 53% more likely to end their marriage. According to the Australian paper, age differences, either way, are associated with advanced threats, especially if the man is young. The study suggests it may be" due to differences in values associated with birth control, or connubial strain caused by power imbalances within the union."

23. Someone thinks they are always right.

Suppose you are smarter than your partner. By far, the biggest predictors of divorce are set up in couples' stations to each other. Famed experimenter John Gottman claims to be suitable to prognosticate a couple's chances with 93 delicacies, grounded on four crucial traits which include being protective and constant review. But he says the" kiss of death," is disdain and seeing your mate as beneath you.

" It's constant wrathfulness and nausea, unresistant-aggressive lodgings, eye-rolling, and yelling at your mate," says Sussman." When couples do that in a session, I say the exploration shows that if you keep doing that, there is a really good chance you are going to get disassociated."

Chapter 5: RESOLVING MARRIAGE PROBLEMS

When faced with a difference in opinion, we may get protective about our views and occasionally hurt and put the other party down in the process. This can be mischievous to any connubial relationship, especially in the long run. How also can you resolve conflicts amicably with your partner rather than fighting it out over a heated argument?

Feelings can and do run grandly during a disagreement. But rather than raising your voice and pointing fritters, it would help to reuse and talk through your passions with your partner. Keep the tone of your voice in check. Try to exercise collective respect and tone-control while addressing an issue.

What numerous people tend to do during conflicts is to keep a record of the other party's historical wrongdoings and use it against them. Bringing in once and unconnected events don't help with resolving the issue at hand and should be avoided at all cost. espousing a ' give- and- take, agreeing- to differ ' approach might be a better way to sustain a relationship in the long run.

Also, taking time- eschewal, when an argument gets too heated and exercising remission, are some ways to help a marriage thrive in the long run.

Couples can try these strategies to resolve their conflicts

- Choosing one issue

Still, pick the most burning issue to work on, If numerous issues arise.

- Communicate for results

This stage is where the couple will communicate and come up with possible results to the said problem.

- Agree on a result

The couple will also decide on the most feasible result and plan when and how to execute it.

- Do Carry out the result

This is the action through which the couple will carry out the resulting plan.

- Follow- up

The couple will also take time to follow- up and review the named result workshop.

Most importantly, when conflicts feel too important to handle, concentrate on your partner's positive attributes and remind yourself of why you first fell in love with your partner and got married. In this marriage, both of you're a platoon and this platoon can work towards a palm-palm situation in any given circumstance. To make your relationship, make it a point to affirm and appreciate your partner daily for the numerous good effects in him or her that are occasionally taken for granted.

Flashback, no one is perfect and having dissensions in a relationship is ineluctable. There's always room for conciliation when effects go awry between a couple. It

takes maturity, time and trouble to work through issues. Don't give in to pride, or allow wrathfulness and conflict to destroy your marriage.
Resolving, we take a break, If we can not compromise. Occasionally we may have to readdress a conflict many times, or give it a day or so; it depends on the issue. The key is to be regardful, loving, open inclined, and true to yourself. The little secret that will help you help conflicts in your marriage. Find. The. Root. Beget! And break it! Don’t let the commodity that's bothering your mold.
You'll have to stop checking Facebook, Twitter, Pinterest, or other social media accounts and spend time with your partner talking about the issues affecting your marriage, family, conflicts, and heated arguments.
Don’t keep it all in by avoiding dealing with your issues head-on. Always be looking for ways to ameliorate your marriage.
Ask your partner, “ What did you mean by this? I know you didn’t mean to hurt me but, I felt X when you said Y or did. ”

More ways on how to resolve conflicts

1. Have an open mind.

Drop any preconceived sundries you have that will help you from talking, agitating, and resolving conflicts with your partner.

2. Commit to working on the conflict or problem you have.

This commitment alone shows you're keen on resolving conflicts in your marriage.

3. Pay attention and hear when your partner is talking.

Don’t be hostile! You want to be heard while talking to your partner, so why not do the same for your partner? Exercise compassionate listening, and try to understand it from your soak’s point of view, not that you have to agree.

4. Identify the root cause of the conflict.

And have a clear understanding of the conflict before trying to resolve it. Without knowing the cause of your conflicts, it'll be veritably delicate to resolve them irrespective of what way or plan you take.

5. Take responsibility for your conduct and feelings.

Don’t be protective of them, be responsible.

6. Be willing to forgive your partner, or ask for remission.

7. Find results, and concession(a common ground) and apply the results you both agreed upon. Take action!

8. Suppose it is a palm for both of you.

In marriage, one partner doesn't win while the other loses, you either win or lose together.There you have it, no further defenses for fighting and arguing about your conflicts. It’s about time you resolved them with your partner.

How to talk about it.

See where you both agree on commodities and use your differences to ameliorate your marriage.

Figure out a plan that will help you, and your partner resolve conflicts in your marriage. For illustration, we don't buy any precious item(s) unless we talk it over with each other and agree!

www.ingramcontent.com/pod-product-compliance
Lightning Source LLC
LaVergne TN
LVHW020529160826
845677LV00015B/3982